You are made of
STARS

Inspirational Quotes
Coloring Book

Illustrated by Forest Diver

www.JuliaRivers.com

When was the last time you did something

for the

FIRST TIME?

Everybody wants happiness,
nobody wants pain,
but you can't have a rainbow
without a little rain.

THINK
lovely wonderful thoughts...
THEY LIFT YOU UP IN THE AIR

Coloring Books

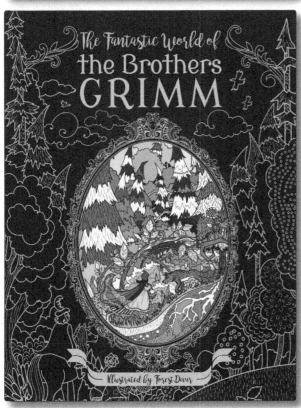

Lovin' the Good Vibes
A Happiness Coloring Book
MISTAKES are proof
that you are Trying
Illustrated by Lily Chloe

ALICE'S ADVENTURES IN WONDERLAND
Illustrated by forest Diver
Drink Me

FAIRY TALES DOODLE ADVENTURE
Illustrated by Ronie C. Pios

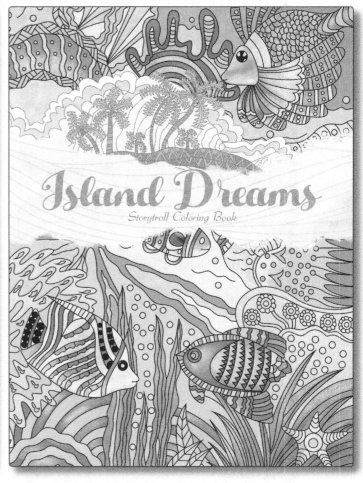

Island Dreams
Storytroll Coloring Book

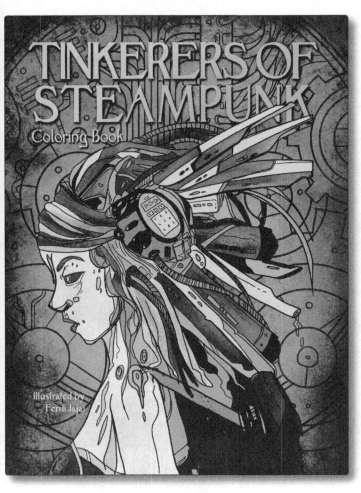

The Book of Phantastical
Dragons
Storytroll Coloring Book

Storytroll Coloring Book
Impressions of Spring

Illustrated by MgA. Radana Planka

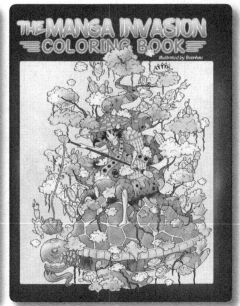

THE MANGA INVASION COLORING BOOK
Illustrated by Boonhau

Coloring Book
Majestic Nature
Illustrated by Ika Sirana

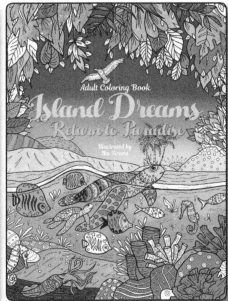

Adult Coloring Book
Island Dreams
Return to Paradise
Illustrated by
Ika Sirana

DINOMON
Invasion of the
Dinosaur Doodles

Illustrated by Ruric C. Poo

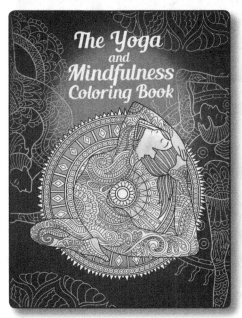

The Yoga
and
Mindfulness
Coloring Book

Storytroll Studios
Fantastic Ocean
Coloring Book

Illustrated by Ksenia Spirina

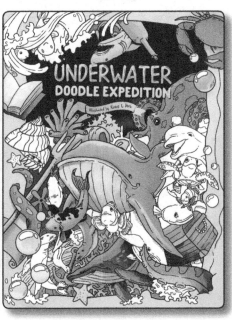

**UNDERWATER
DOODLE EXPEDITION**

Illustrated by Ruric C. Poo

Children's Books

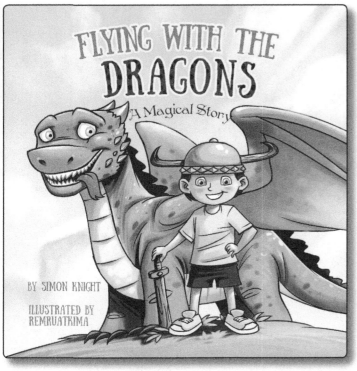

17583498R00044